ALMIGHTY GOD, WHOSE BLESSED APOSTLES

PETER AND PAUL GLORIFIED THEE BY

THEIR MARTYRDOM: GRANT THAT THY CHURCH,

INSTRUCTED BY THEIR TEACHING AND

EXAMPLE, AND KNIT TOGETHER IN UNITY BY

THY SPIRIT, MAY EVER STAND FIRM UPON

THE ONE FOUNDATION, WHICH IS JESUS CHRIST

OUR LORD; WHO LIVETH AND REIGNETH

WITH THEE, IN THE UNITY OF THE SAME SPIRIT,

ONE GOD, FOR EVER AND EVER. AMEN

COLLECT FOR SAINT PETER AND SAINT PAUL, FROM
THE BOOK OF COMMON PRAYER

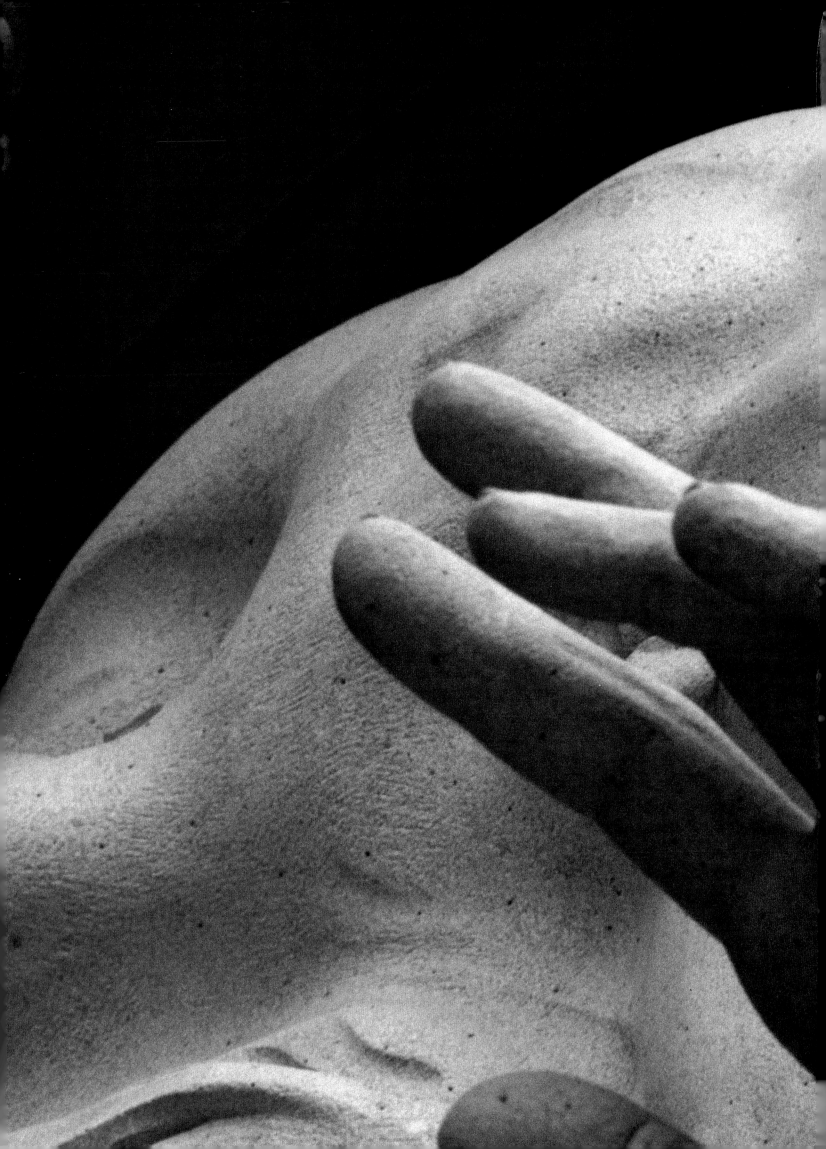

Designed by Marilyn Appleby
Edited by Kathleen D. Valenzi, with the assistance of Ross A.
Howell Jr., Stephanie A. Lear, and Shirita E. Hawks.
Photography copyright © 1988 by Robert Llewellyn. All rights reserved.
Introduction copyright © 1988 by John Chancellor. All rights reserved.
This book, or any portions thereof, may not be reproduced
or transmitted in any form or by any means, electronic or mechanical,
including photocopying, recording, or by any information storage and
retrieval system, without permission in writing from the publisher.
Photography may not be reproduced without permission of Robert Llewellyn.
The introduction may not be reproduced without permission of John Chancellor.
Library of Congress Catalog Card Number 88-80088
ISBN 0-943231-07-8
Printed and bound in Hong Kong by Everbest Printing.
Published by Howell Press, Inc., 1147 River Road, Bay 2,
Charlottesville, Virginia 22901. Telephone 804-977-4006.
Second printing 1992

HOWELL PRESS

THE CATHEDRAL

OF SAINT PETER AND SAINT PAUL

PHOTOGRAPHY BY ROBERT LLEWELLYN

INTRODUCTION BY JOHN CHANCELLOR

A National Church

IT IS THERE, off the wing, as the plane turns into the final approach down the Potomac. Of all things. A 14th-century cathedral, sparkling gray and silver in the sunlight, improbable and fantastic, set in a 20th-century landscape of satellite dishes and television towers. What is a Gothic masterpiece doing there, high above a city where the lowest bidders usually set the architectural standards?

It is the Protestant Episcopal Cathedral Church of St. Peter and St. Paul, known to millions as the Washington Cathedral, a house of worship for all, a national church in the nation's capital.

The United States was the first country in the Christian era to plan and build its capital city. The plan drawn up by Major Pierre Charles L'Enfant was commissioned by President Washington. L'Enfant proposed "a great church for national purposes." But the young Republic drew a strong line between religion and the state, so that church was never built. In fact much of L'Enfant's plan was ignored in those bustling days of new nationhood, and the plan itself was, incredibly, lost. Almost a century later the "Plan for the City of Washington" was discovered in the files of the Geodetic Survey, and the dreams of Washington and L'Enfant began to be realized. In the early years of this century, the Congress drew up plans for parks, the railroad tracks along the Mall were removed, the Capitol grounds were terraced, and Union Station was built. Yet there was no Congressional proposal for "a great church for national purposes."

Other religious groups founded schools in the capital during the last century: Catholic University and the American University of the Methodists. And in 1893 the Congress chartered the Protestant Episcopal Cathedral Foundation and empowered it to build a cathedral and establish schools "for the promotion of religion and education and charity." It was a splendid charter, signed by President Benjamin Harrison, but there was no money, no land, and not even an Episcopal Diocese of Washington.

There was, however, a small Episcopal church on Alban Hill in northwest Washington, rather far, in those days, from the center of the city. St. Alban's Church had been consecrated in 1854 as the first free church in the District of Columbia. The Washington Cathedral was built around that property. Had the little church not been there in the beginning, the big church might be somewhere else today.

Under the tireless leadership of the first Episcopal Bishop of Washington, the Reverend Dr. Henry Yates Satterlee, money was found to purchase 57 acres on Alban Hill, a magnificent site overlooking the city. It is now called Mount Saint Alban. Much of the money came from the rich, but Bishop Satterlee offered Founder's Certificates to anyone who gave a dollar. He envisioned the cathedral as a "...spiritual home to which men of every class, rich and poor, statesman, tradesman and laborer, may come without money and without price, with the consciousness that it is their Father's house." That, precisely, is the philosophy of the cathedral today.

Every president since Harrison has had some association with the cathedral. At the end of the Spanish-American War, President McKinley drove up from the White House to attend dedication ceremonies for the Peace Cross that was raised near St. Alban's Church.

There was no building, not even an excavation, but Bishop Satterlee envisioned the occasion as the first cathedral service. Clergy from all across the country attended.

President Theodore Roosevelt attended the laying of the foundation stone in 1907. Bishop Satterlee used the silver trowel and wooden mallet that President Washington used when the cornerstone of the U.S. Capitol was laid in 1793. Ten thousand people came to the ceremony. The Marine Band played. Roosevelt wished the bishop and his associates "God-speed in the work begun this day."

But a cathedral is not built in a day, a year, or a decade. The cathedral at Rheims, France, took two and a half centuries to build. Exeter, in England, took 99 years. The Washington Cathedral will have taken 83 years, when it is consecrated in 1990. It is the sixth-largest cathedral in the world, larger than Chartres or Notre Dame. From the West Facade to the buttresses on the East, it is almost as long as two football fields; the central tower is more than 20 stories high; the Nave is half again as high as the one in Westminster Abbey, England's tallest medieval vault.

It is a pure 14th-century, English-Gothic cathedral, in the Decorated or Middle-Pointed style. For a time in the 1890s, there was talk of building in the Renaissance style, but Bishop Satterlee's mind was made up. He wanted, he wrote, "a *genuine* Gothic Cathedral on this side of the Atlantic, which will kindle the same religious, devotional feelings and historic associations which are awakened in the breasts of American travellers by the great Gothic cathedrals of Europe." He continued, "American churchmen are so weary of designs which glorify the originality of the architect, that they are longing more and more for a pure Gothic church which is built simply for the glory of God." And so it came to pass. Many architects would be associated with the cathedral and would leave their mark on it, but the essentials of the design had been fixed by the builders of the great cathedrals of Europe and Britain 500 years ago.

A word about Satterlee, a remarkable man. Reading the history of the Washington Cathedral leads me to believe that he was, among many who made this church a reality, the one essential person. When he was asked to become Bishop of Washington, he had served for 14 years as rector of New York City's Calvary Church. He had been elected Bishop of Ohio, then Bishop of Michigan, and had declined both positions.

Satterlee did come to Washington for four reasons, which he outlined in his memoirs. First was his belief in the separation of church and state. He wanted to bring that principle to the creation of a diocese in the capital of the United States. Second was his commitment to mission work among blacks in Washington, D.C., where North and South meet. Third, he wanted to mold the new diocese of Washington on the lines of the primitive, undivided Church, to promote the cause of American Christian and Church unity. And fourth, he felt it was important to make the Cathedral a center of diocesan life. He saw the great church as a witness to the faith of Jesus Christ in the nation's capital.

The terms we use now to describe Bishop Satterlee's beliefs are: religious, ecumenical, socially conscious, and reflective of national life. They remain the priorities of the ministry he began in 1896.

It has not always been easy, this construction of a great cathedral. There were times when building the enormous edifice seemed impossible. In 1919 after the exertions of World War I, work stopped. The stock market crash of 1929 slowed things down. The Depression didn't help. When World War II came along, there were disruptions. The worst financial crisis of all came in the mid-1970s, when *The New York Times* reported that the cathedral was near bankruptcy. In 1977 there was worry that employees might not be paid. It took serious surgery to avoid a financial collapse; costs were cut, construction slowed down, the cathedral survived, and the work of finishing the church continued.

The cathedral has to do all this on its own. It gets no dollars from the U.S. government. It gets no institutional church money for its building fund. It is a church that sits on its own bottom, financially. A recent study showed contributions from people of many religions; 58 percent of its support came from Episcopalians, with sizable support from Presbyterians, Methodists, and Lutherans. On the ironwork screen in the Chapel of the Holy Spirit, there is an inscription that reads, "With God Nothing Shall Be Impossible." True, but friends help a lot. This soaring church could not have been built in its nearly infinite detail without the generous support of private citizens of all faiths.

And if God, as someone said, can be found in the details, this cathedral is truly blessed. Gothic architecture is what has been called "ordered freedom." This is the joyous custom of encouraging craftsmen to express themselves within defined limits. Stonecarvers, wood workers, iron workers must produce objects that fit, that work, that are harmonious with the design of the cathedral. But within those ordered boundaries, the designs themselves are the product of the creative, and collaborative, imagination of sculptor and stonecarver. Hence the magnificent array of carved rosettes, crockets, finials,

trefoils, ball flowers, dentils, and stylized leaves, all different, all original. There are thousands, everywhere. On the central tower there are 732 hand-carved crockets, 84 finials, and 400 other carvings. There are also 96 carved angels. Each angel is different.

In their book on the Washington Cathedral *To Thy Great Glory*, Richard T. Feller and Marshall W. Fishwick wrote of Gothic carvings, "Over the centuries they have evolved into their own abstractions. Being conventionalized they are seldom seen and noticed by the casual eye. They break up the long lines, create the lights and shadows. They add the interest and softness not found on the modern flat-surface wall. These carvings allow freedom without confusion, sequence without monotony, imitation without idolatry."

Gargoyles and grotesques are functional. Gargoyles carry rainwater away from stone walls through their mouths; grotesques deflect the water with their heads or tongues. The hideous face or the demonic visage is the result of a creative interplay between sculptor and stonecarver. This is an art that is eight centuries old, but some of it is refreshingly contemporary. Ninety-five feet above the floor of the South Transept is a four-foot-wide relief of a modern family singing praises to the Lord. Some of it is funny. The faces of neighborhood dogs are carved on one of the flying buttresses. The church mouse and the church cat are carved in the North Transept. One column in the church is topped by two small, carved figures; they are architects. One is scratching his head in perplexity, while the other raises a finger to say, "I have found the solution!" There is glorious woodcarving in this cathedral. An armrest on a pew depicts Noah's Ark on a boiling sea. The Bishop's stall is a masterpiece which evokes the finest work of the

Middle Ages. Wrought-iron workers, mosaicists, silversmiths, even needlepoint artists have added their skills to the incredible richness of the cathedral. Some of the finest sculptors and stained-glass artists in the world have given it greatness.

Were it not for the labors of these talented people, the cathedral would be beautiful but dull. For eight decades, they have been at work, and it was sometimes hard to keep them, to train them, and even, occasionally, to pay them. The cathedral has mourned some of them; one master stonecutter fell to his death from a high scaffold in the Nave in 1955. Yet when the Cathedral Church of St. Peter and St. Paul is finished, it will have more statuary than the Cathedral of Chartres.

Although the architecture of the cathedral is classically Gothic, it is emphatically an American church. Evidence of this is everywhere. A mosaic of 50 state seals is set in the floor inside the West entrance, with the Great Seal of the United States in the center. In the Nave the Washington Bay honors the first president. The Folger Bay celebrates symbols of America: the eagle, bison, wild turkeys — and explorers Lewis and Clark. One bay is dedicated to the memory of Charles Warren, historian of the Supreme Court. Warren was a native of Massachusetts, which is represented by a stained-glass codfish. There is a bay honoring the memory of Generals Robert E. Lee and Stonewall Jackson. The oak screens in the War Memorial Chapel were given by the U.S. Marines. President Wilson, Admiral Dewey, Helen Keller, and more than 140 other Americans are interred in this cathedral. In St. John's Chapel there are individual needlepoint kneelers, each dedicated to someone prominent in American history: Herman Melville, Alexander Graham Bell, Robert Fulton, Harriet Tubman, John F. Kennedy.

An American church. A national church. A place for a nation to mourn its fallen and praise its living. A church for state funerals and vigils for national remembrance. A forum for the discussion of issues of the day. The Reverend Martin Luther King Jr. delivered his Sunday sermon in the cathedral four days before his death. The wall between church and state still stands in the United States, but the need for L'Enfant's "great church for national purposes" is fulfilled by the Washington Cathedral.

Three-hundred thousand visitors a year pass through its portals, welcomed and guided by a battalion of volunteers. The All Hallows Guild cares for the landscaping. There are volunteer archivists, bell ringers, vergers, lay readers, ushers, aides, even a Needlepoint Committee, all honored to be part of this magnificent enterprise.

Why does the cathedral have so many friends? I am one. What is it about this supreme anachronism that draws me to it? Perhaps because it is not an anachronism, not out of step with its time. When the age of Gothic cathedrals began 800 years ago, most people could neither read nor write. It's been said that the Gothic style, with its soaring vaults and fantastic embellishments, was the mass media of its time. People didn't have to be able to read or write to get pleasure — indeed, thrills — out of their cathedral. A visit to the Cathedral of Chartres in the 13th century was prime-time medieval entertainment as much as religious obligation.

Yet today, a visit to the Washington Cathedral provides pleasure, and thrills, to people made dizzy by too much 20th-century communication. I think that's because the message of a church of this kind depends not upon reading or writing but upon the heart; the message is deeper than words or pictures. Henry Adams wrote of

Chartres, "Like all great churches, that are not mere storehouses of theology, Chartres expressed, whatever else it meant, an emotion, the deepest man ever felt, the struggle of his own littleness to grasp the infinite." That gets close to my own feeling when I see the cathedral, marvel at its size, enter the Nave—I can't grasp the infinite, but being there allows me to acknowledge its existence.

For some years we lived in a house within sound of the cathedral bells. My son went to school there and sang in the choir. Our family strolled through its grounds, husband, wife, children, dog. We played in the Bishop's Garden. Listened to choristers in the east cloister. Bought Christmas trees and wreaths at the greenhouse. Shopped in the Herb Cottage. The place was woven into our lives. The cathedral dominated our neighborhood, but its size was not oppressive. Instead, it gave us, literally, something to look up to. It gave me a sense of permanence. It made me believe that the cycles of life, of birth, family, and death were ordered and natural. Our lives would come and go while the great church would remain, a symbol of the eternal God. That was a lesson taught by these stones and statues.

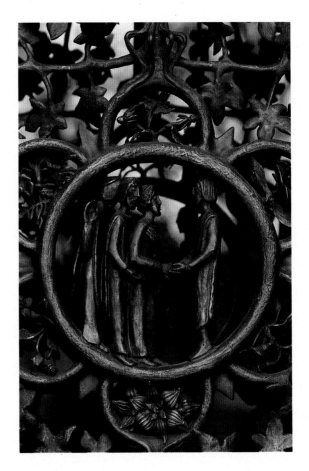

I have often wondered if my feeling for my cathedral matches the feeling of a medieval man for his. I think it does. That citizen of Chartres or Exeter is my spiritual kinsman. Both of us have received messages deeper than words. Cathedrals do that. It seems to me that no other structures built by man communicate on such a fundamental level.

I'm not sure anyone will build a great Gothic cathedral again, the way the world is going. So it is our good fortune to have this book, and Robert Llewellyn's memorable photographs, which so beautifully capture the spirit of this holy edifice.

John Chancellor

JESUS, WALKING BY THE SEA OF GALILEE, SAW

TWO BRETHREN, SIMON CALLED PETER,

AND ANDREW HIS BROTHER, CASTING A NET

INTO THE SEA: FOR THEY WERE FISHERS.

AND HE SAITH UNTO THEM, FOLLOW ME, AND I

WILL MAKE YOU FISHERS OF MEN.

AND THEY STRAIGHTAWAY LEFT THEIR NETS,

AND FOLLOWED HIM.

MATTHEW 4:18-20

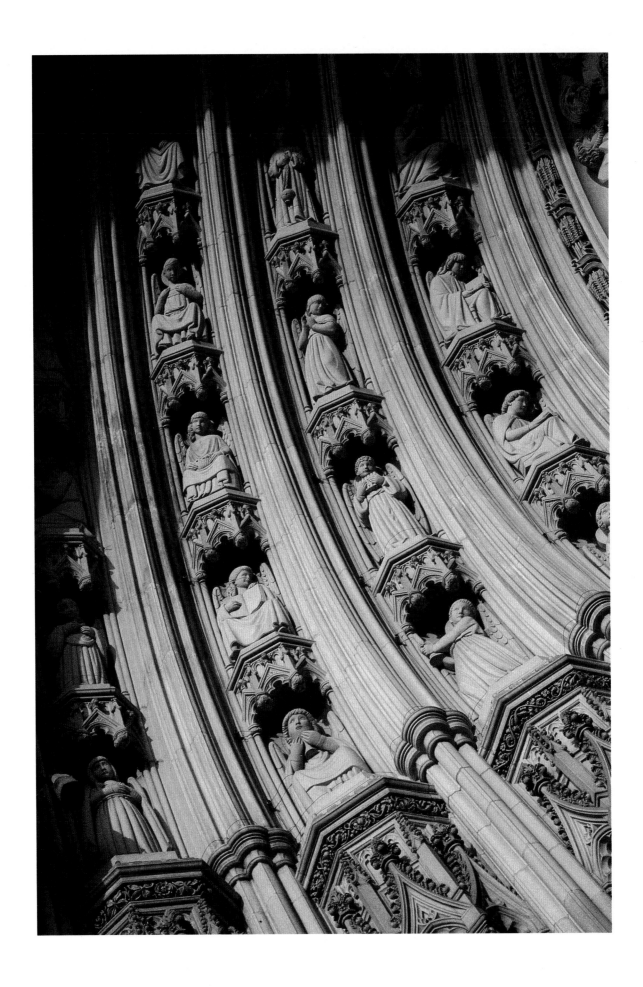

I WAS GLAD WHEN THEY SAID UNTO ME,

LET US GO INTO THE HOUSE

OF THE LORD.

PSALMS 122:1

FOR NOW WE SEE THROUGH A GLASS,

DARKLY; BUT THEN FACE TO FACE.

I CORINTHIANS 13:12

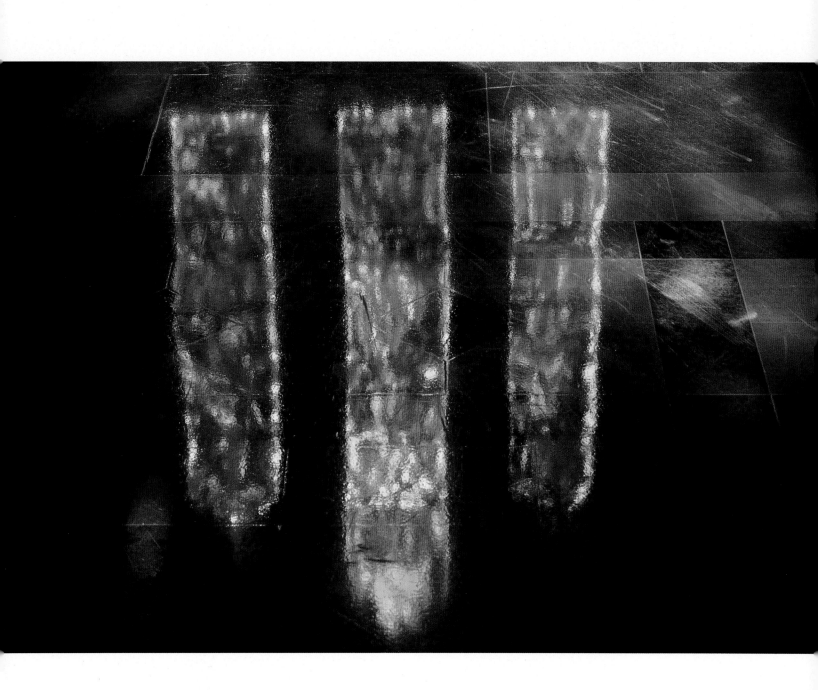

ASK, AND IT SHALL BE GIVEN YOU; SEEK,
AND YE SHALL FIND; KNOCK, AND IT
SHALL BE OPENED UNTO YOU.

MATTHEW 7:7

BEHOLD, A VIRGIN SHALL BE WITH CHILD,

AND SHALL BRING FORTH A SON, AND

THEY SHALL CALL HIS NAME EMMANUEL,

WHICH BEING INTERPRETED IS,

GOD WITH US.

MATTHEW 1:23

BE FILLED WITH THE SPIRIT;
SPEAKING TO YOURSELVES IN PSALMS
AND HYMNS AND SPIRITUAL SONGS,
SINGING AND MAKING MELODY IN YOUR
HEART TO THE LORD.

EPHESIANS 5:18-19

BLESSED ARE THE POOR IN SPIRIT: FOR THEIRS IS

THE KINGDOM OF HEAVEN.

BLESSED ARE THEY THAT MOURN: FOR THEY SHALL

BE COMFORTED.

BLESSED ARE THE MEEK: FOR THEY SHALL INHERIT

THE EARTH.

BLESSED ARE THEY WHICH DO HUNGER AND

THIRST AFTER RIGHTEOUSNESS:

FOR THEY SHALL BE FILLED.

BLESSED ARE THE MERCIFUL: FOR THEY SHALL

OBTAIN MERCY.

BLESSED ARE THE PURE IN HEART: FOR THEY

SHALL SEE GOD.

BLESSED ARE THE PEACEMAKERS: FOR THEY SHALL

BE CALLED THE CHILDREN OF GOD.

MATTHEW 5:3-9

FAITH IS THE SUBSTANCE OF THINGS
HOPED FOR, THE EVIDENCE OF
THINGS NOT SEEN.

HEBREWS 2:1

WHAT IS MAN, THAT THOU ART MINDFUL OF

HIM? AND THE SON OF MAN, THAT THOU

VISITEST HIM?

FOR THOU HAST MADE HIM A LITTLE LOWER

THAN THE ANGELS, AND HAST CROWNED

HIM WITH GLORY AND HONOUR.

PSALMS 8:4-5

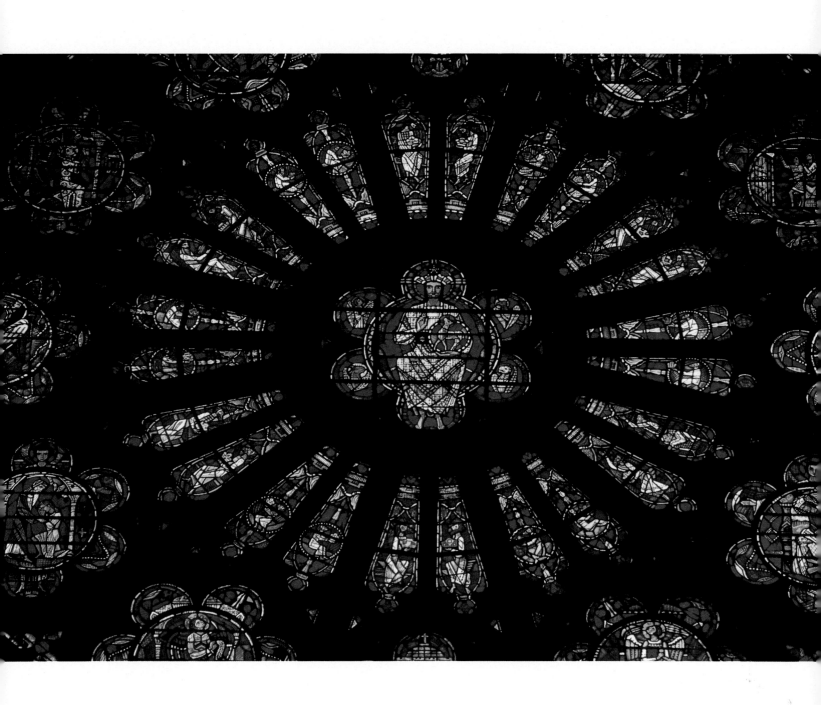

AS A SHEPHERD SEEKETH OUT HIS FLOCK IN

THE DAY THAT HE IS AMONG HIS SHEEP THAT

ARE SCATTERED; SO WILL I SEEK OUT MY

SHEEP, AND WILL DELIVER THEM OUT OF

ALL PLACES WHERE THEY HAVE BEEN

SCATTERED IN THE CLOUDY AND DARK DAY.

EZEKIEL 34:12

O LORD, HOW MANIFOLD ARE THY WORKS!

IN WISDOM HAST THOU MADE THEM ALL:

THE EARTH IS FULL OF THY RICHES.

PSALMS 104:24

COME UNTO ME, ALL YE THAT LABOUR AND ARE

HEAVY LADEN, AND I WILL GIVE YOU REST.

TAKE MY YOKE UPON YOU, AND LEARN OF ME;

FOR I AM MEEK AND LOWLY IN HEART:

AND YE SHALL FIND REST UNTO YOUR SOULS.

FOR MY YOKE IS EASY, AND MY BURDEN IS LIGHT.

MATTHEW 11:28-30

LET THE HEAVENS BE GLAD,

AND LET THE EARTH REJOICE: AND LET

MEN SAY AMONG THE NATIONS,

THE LORD REIGNETH.

I CHRONICLES 16:31

FOR MINE HOUSE SHALL BE CALLED AN

HOUSE OF PRAYER FOR ALL PEOPLE.

ISAIAH 56:7

THIS IS THE DAY WHICH THE LORD

HATH MADE; WE WILL REJOICE AND

BE GLAD IN IT.

PSALMS 118:24

THE LORD IS MY STRENGTH AND SONG,

AND HE IS BECOME MY SALVATION:

HE IS MY GOD, AND I WILL PREPARE HIM

AN HABITATION; MY FATHER'S GOD,

AND I WILL EXALT HIM.

EXODUS 15:2

THE LORD IS IN HIS HOLY TEMPLE: LET ALL

THE EARTH KEEP SILENCE BEFORE HIM.

HABAKKUK 2:20

THEN SPAKE THE LORD TO PAUL IN THE NIGHT

BY A VISION, BE NOT AFRAID, BUT SPEAK,

AND HOLD NOT THY PEACE.

ACTS 18:9

NOTES

2-3

DETAIL, *ADAM*, WEST FACADE. The theme of the west facade is creation. *Adam* was designed by sculptor Frederick E. Hart.

4-5

THE CREATION, WEST FACADE. Rowan LeCompte's rose window portrays the creation of light as described in the Book of Genesis. Rose windows are cousins to Romanesque wheel windows that symbolize the basic unity of the Godhead.

6-7

APSE. In 1908 architect Henry Vaughan modified cathedral plans by omitting the ambulatory, or closed passageway, that was to be built behind the sanctuary. Doing so permitted additional light into the Bethlehem Chapel, which is located beneath the sanctuary at the crypt-floor level, and resulted in one of the few examples of free-standing flying buttresses.

8-9

ACOLYTES, NAVE CENTER AISLE. The marble and slate floors of the cathedral were designed by architect Philip Hubert Frohman, who worked for 51 years on the edifice. Quarries in Vermont, Tennessee, Maryland, and Italy provided the different pieces of colored marble.

10

ANGEL, SOUTH PORTAL VOUSSOIR. Spanish artist Enrique Monjo produced the models for the 44 voussoir angels, and over a four-and-a-half-year period, Roger Morigi and Frank Zic carved them. A voussoir is the ring of stones forming an arch.

12

SOUTH TRANSEPT AND GLORIA IN EXCELSIS TOWER. Once construction of the 301-foot central tower was begun, it rose at the rate of one foot per day. Workmen raised the scaffolding each day to match the current height of the tower.

17

DETAIL, BRONZE GATE, SAINT PAUL PORTAL.

18-19

CREATION, WEST PORTAL TYMPANUM. Designed by Frederick E. Hart, the relief carving depicts the formation of mankind from a void.

20

SAINT PETER, WEST FACADE.

22

ANGELS, SOUTH PORTAL VOUSSOIR. Because of the intricacy of their design, the canopies above the 44 angels took more time to carve than the angels themselves.

23

THE CHOIR. Most boys begin training for positions on the Cathedral Choir of Men and Boys when they are seven or eight years old and continue until their voices change with the onset of puberty.

25

NAVE, LOOKING TOWARD HIGH ALTAR. The 12 stones for the High Altar came from the "quarries of Solomon" that once provided the stone for King Solomon's temple.

26-27

GOTHIC ARCHES NEAR ST. JOHN'S CHAPEL REREDOS.

28

JOB. The tormented figure of Job, shown in the lancet to the left of center, symbolizes faith and suffering. He looks longingly at a child, who represents hope and new life, in the arms of the Good Shepherd. The many white crosses and stars of David scattered throughout the window pay tribute to American military dead.

29

PSALMS. The figures shown are symbolic of the four major Psalter motifs: (left to right) "Thanksgiving," "Praise," "Supplication," and "Lamentation."

31

DETAIL, *ISAIAH*. An angel, bending down to touch the lips of Isaiah with a hot coal, absolves the Hebrew prophet of his sins.

32

THE GREAT ORGAN. Designed and built by Ernest M. Skinner, the Great Organ contained 8,311 pipes when it was completed in 1938. Since then new pipes have been added, bringing the total to 10,323.

33

RELIGIOUS FREEDOM IN MARYLAND REFLECTIONS. This stained-glass window commemorates the Act of Toleration, passed by the Maryland General Assembly in 1649. This act fostered the efforts of major Christian groups to live together in peace and harmony.

34

APSE, NORTH TRANSEPT, AND CATHEDRAL OFFICES (lower left). In his plans for the nation's capital, French engineer Pierre Charles L'Enfant included land for a great national church open to all people. Although L'Enfant's church never materialized, the idea of a house of prayer for all people was embodied in the charter of the cathedral foundation enacted by the U.S. Congress in 1893.

35

BETHLEHEM CHAPEL. The Gothic-style chapel was the first part of the cathedral to be built.

36

STAIRWAY, RESURRECTION CHAPEL. The Bethlehem,

Cornerstone ceremony, 1907.

St. Joseph of Arimathea, and Resurrection chapels on the crypt level of the cathedral relate the major events in the life of Christ: his birth, death, and rising again.

37

DETAIL, *THE RISEN CHRIST MOSAIC,* RESURRECTION CHAPEL. Of Norman design, the chapel is filled with colorful mosaics. These multi-tiled artforms were common adornments in Byzantine churches and were incorporated into Romanesque architecture in the 11th and 12th centuries.

38-39

DETAIL, *THE RISEN CHRIST MOSAIC,* RESURRECTION CHAPEL. The hands shown are those of an angel, kneeling before Christ's open tomb.

40-41

BISHOP JAMES HANNINGTON OF AFRICA, ST. ALBAN OF BRITAIN, AND *ST. STEPHEN OF HUNGARY,* HIGH ALTAR REREDOS. The three figures, named left to right, are carved of Caen stone, which has a warmer hue than limestone. The term "reredos" applies to the carved wall or screen found at the back of an altar.

42

PORTAL, WEST FACADE. Former Bishop of Washington Henry Yates Satterlee desired "a *genuine* Gothic cathedral on this side of the Atlantic." His tireless efforts toward attaining this goal resulted in the establishment of the Protestant Episcopal Cathedral Foundation on January 6, 1893.

43

DETAIL, CHOIR PRACTICE ROOM WINDOW. Since 1912, when the first service was held in the cathedral, the Cathedral Choir of Men and Boys has sung for the congregation. The boys, who start out by training with the Chapel Choir, compete for positions on the prestigious senior choir.

44-45

SERVICE AT THE CROSSING.

46-47

PINNACLES. Each pinnacle is decorated with small, leaf-like ornaments called crockets and topped by a carved finial. The faces of the prophets look out from the bottom of the right-hand pinnacle.

49

DETAIL, SAINT MARY'S CHAPEL REREDOS. Carved of linden wood by Ernest Pellegrini, the polychromed reredos shows Mary offering Jesus to the world.

50

CHRISTMAS PAGEANT, THE CROSSING. The Crossing, which serves as the location for many activities besides religious services, has been the world premiere site for operas by Gian Carlo Menotti and John La Montaine.

51

CHRISTMAS PAGEANT, THE CROSSING.

52

VISITING CHOIR, THE CROSSING. A Jerusalem Cross, originally the Coat of Arms of Godfrey of Bouillon, was adopted as the cathedral's cross by Bishop Henry Yates Satterlee to symbolize the Christian line of descent from the early church of Jerusalem. Also called a Crusader's Cross, a Jerusalem Cross is inlaid in marble on the floor of the crossing.

53

COLLEGE OF PREACHERS (foreground), CATHEDRAL, AND NATIONAL CATHEDRAL SCHOOL (upper right). The cathedral complex includes three schools, two colleges, gardens, and the cathedral itself on 57 acres atop Washington's highest point.

55

FREDERICK WARD DENYS TOMB AND SARCOPHAGUS, RESURRECTION CHAPEL ANTE-CHAPEL.

56

APSE AND GLORIA IN EXCELSIS TOWER. Louis IX of France once said that "a cathedral is a form of thanksgiving; it offers God creativity in the Christian spirit."

Stonecarver, 1923.

57

VOTIVE CANDLES, HOLY SPIRIT CHAPEL. The dove, a symbol of the Holy Spirit, is a major theme in this chapel devoted to private prayer and meditation.

58-59

CHAPEL OF ST. JOSEPH OF ARIMATHEA. The chapel, shaped in the form of a Greek cross, contains the cathedral's only mural. It was painted by Polish emigrant Jan Henryk de Rosen, who used members of the cathedral choir as models.

60

NAVE VAULTING.

61

HOLY EUCHARIST AT THE CATHEDRAL. Over 1,500 services take place at the cathedral annually. Amongst these have been a thanksgiving service for American hostages in Iran on January 29, 1981, and a round-the-clock reading of the names of those killed in Vietnam as part of dedication ceremonies for the Vietnam War Memorial in 1982.

62

CHRIST IN MAJESTY, TER SANCTUS REREDOS. Located behind the High Altar, the *Ter Sanctus*—"thrice holy"—reredos contains carvings of men and women who lived their lives in full accordance with the Christian faith. Four models for the majestus figure were sculpted and tried before one was placed permanently in 1973.

63

ALTAR CROSS, ST. MARY'S CHAPEL.

64

STAINED-GLASS REFLECTIONS, MAIN ARCADE ARCHES.

Easter Sunday, 1933.

Aerial view of the Apse, 1935.

65

ST. MARY'S CHAPEL. Hung on the wall of the chapel are 16th-century Flemish tapestries that relate the story of David and Goliath.

66

SPACE. In 1974 President Nixon directed NASA to give the cathedral a piece of moonrock for use in the center of the *Space* window. To protect the 3-1/2-billion-year-old rock from the Earth's atmosphere, NASA craftsmen sealed it in nitrogen between two pieces of tempered glass, wrapped by a band of stainless steel.

67

THE CHURCH TRIUMPHANT, SOUTH TRANSEPT. Depicting St. John's vision of the throne of God from the Book of Revelation, the south rose window has 12 petals.

68

FLYING BUTTRESSES, APSE. These Gothic supports counteract the outward thrust of cathedral walls and vaulting.

69

THE GOOD SHEPHERD. Designed by Walker Hancock, the sculpture is located in the Chapel of the Good Shepherd, which is open 24 hours a day, year round.

70-71

CATHEDRAL. Like most European cathedrals, the Cathedral of Saint Peter and Saint Paul does not have solid limestone walls because the expense would be prohibitive. A less costly material is used in the core of the walls. For instance, between the 50,000 cubic feet of limestone that make up the walls of the central tower are 1.5 million bricks.

72

SHADOW HOUSE, BISHOP'S GARDEN. Florence Brown Bratenahl, wife of the first cathedral dean, designed the Bishop's Garden, Pilgrim Steps, and the landscaping for the College of Preachers. In 1916 she helped establish the All Hallows Guild to maintain the grounds around the cathedral.

73

BISHOP'S GARDEN. When the foundation stone was dedicated in 1907, 62 bishops and their families assembled for the ceremony. It was the largest turnout of bishops for such an event in the history of the American church.

75

DETAIL, HOLY SPIRIT CHAPEL REREDOS. The figure of Christ in the center of the oak-paneled reredos is the work of noted painter and illustrator N.C. Wyeth.

76

DETAIL, *CREATION ROSE,* WEST FACADE. Cathedral planners wanted windows that would be rich in primary colors. Chunk glass was used along with typical cathedral flat glass to enhance the color and prismatic effect of the great West Rose window.

Telecast of a cathedral service in the 1950s.

77

CATHEDRAL, SOUTH FACADE. Martin Luther King Jr. gave his last Sunday sermon from the cathedral's Canterbury Pulpit on March 31, 1968. Four days later he was assassinated in Memphis, Tennessee.

78

GARGOYLES. "Gargoyle," which comes from *gargouiller*, the French verb for "to gargle," is the name given to the grotesque or whimsically carved waterspouts that project from the gutters of the cathedral's roof.

79

CHRISTMAS PAGEANT, THE CROSSING.

80

VAULTING BOSSES. There are 721 bosses at the cathedral. They are intended to make a pleasing transition at the intersections of the vaulting ribs.

81

CHANCEL VAULTING.

82

DETAIL, THE GEORGE WASHINGTON BAY. When designing the statue of America's first President, artist Lee Lawrie wanted to show George Washington as he might have looked entering Christ Church in Alexandria, Virginia. The monument stands near the entrance to the Rare Book Library.

83

A PIER. The main support for an arch or vault, a pier is usually designed to resemble a number of columns grouped together.

84-85

CENTRAL TOWER, WITH WASHINGTON MONUMENT AND POTOMAC RIVER IN BACKGROUND.

86

DETAIL, HOLY SPIRIT CHAPEL REREDOS.

87

SOUTH TRANSEPT.

88

PORTAL, WEST FACADE.

89

DETAIL, SOUTH PORTAL VOUSSOIR.

90

DETAIL, GLORIA IN EXCELSIS TOWER.

91

GLORIA IN EXCELSIS TOWER. The tower houses the 53-bell Kibbey Carillon and the 10-bell English ring. It is the only cathedral tower in the world that contains both types of bells. Their combined weight is approximately 200 tons.

93

GOTHIC VAULTING. The pedestals from which cathedral vaulting ribs spring upward and outward are called conoids. In medieval times, each conoid was set as a single, large block of stone, and stonemasons would cut ribs into them. Advances in architectural design have made that approach obsolete, and conoids, such as those shown here, are pre-carved at stone-cutting mills before being permanently set.

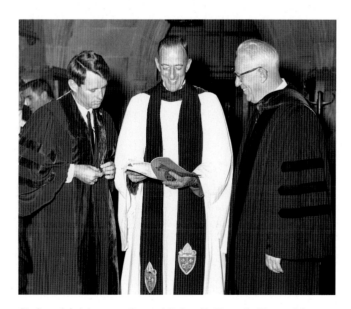

(Left to right) Attorney General Robert F. Kennedy, Dean of the Washington Cathedral Francis B. Sayre, Jr., and Chief Justice Earl Warren at the dedication of the Gloria in Excelsis Tower, 1964.

President Jimmy Carter and Vice President Walter Mondale at a prayer vigil for American hostages in Iran, 1979.

94

DETAIL, BISHOP'S GARDEN STONES. Acquired from abbeys in Europe, these carved stones are of an unknown age.

95

BISHOP'S GARDEN.

96

DETAIL, KIBBEY CARILLON. The bells were cast at the Taylor Bell Foundry in Loughborough, England.

97

GABRIEL, SOUTH TRANSEPT. Many sculptures, such as the archangel *Gabriel*, are located too high up to be seen clearly. Nevertheless, they exhibit flawless detailing, front and back. The desire for perfection on the part of cathedral builders ensures that the object is worthy for the eyes of God.

98-99

SOUTH FACADE.

100

DETAIL, GLORIA IN EXCELSIS TOWER. From the top of the cathedral, an angel looks down upon every gargoyle and grotesque.

101

GARTH. An abstract bronze fountain is located in the garth, the open courtyard of the cloister. Its floral feeling complements the plantings of the garth, and its size keeps it from being overpowered by the massive edifice that surrounds it.

102

FLYING BUTTRESSES.

103

BLIND BARTIMAEUS, SOUTH PORTAL. Depicting the man whose eyesight was restored by Christ on the road out of Jericho, the sculpture was created by Enrique Monjo.

104

CLERGYMAN.

105

DETAIL, ENTRANCE TO AN OUTER AISLE BAY.

106

THE SERVICE.

107

DETAIL, *THE LAST SUPPER*, SOUTH PORTAL TYMPANUM. This bas-relief carving was created by sculptor Heinz Warneke.

108

CATHEDRAL. President Woodrow Wilson was interred in the cathedral after his death in 1924. His grandson, the Very Reverend Francis B. Sayre Jr., served as dean and chairman of the cathedral's building committee from 1951 to 1978.

109

LEAD ROOF, APSE.

110-111

CATHEDRAL, NORTH FACADE.

112

SAINT PAUL, WEST FACADE.

Master Stonecarver Emeritus Roger Morigi with Adam, 1980.

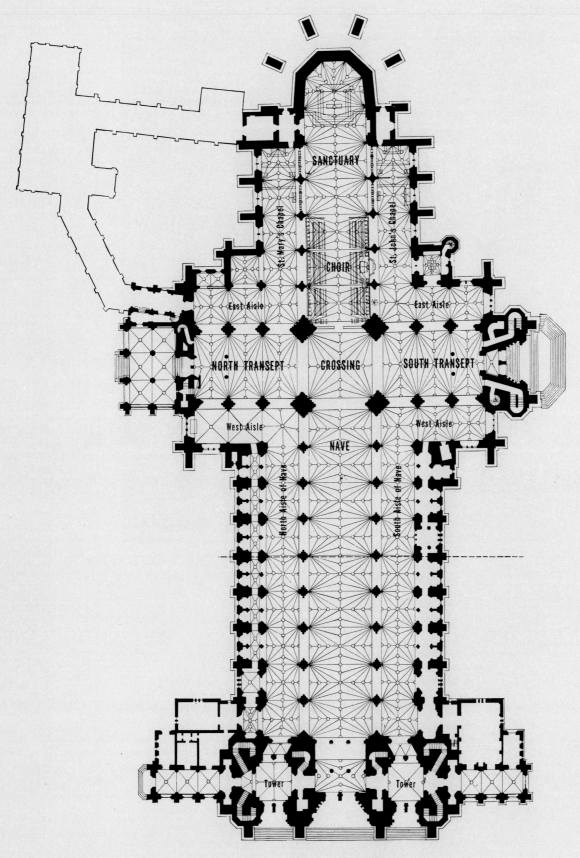

Nave Level Floor Plan.

WEST ELEVATION

West Facade.

The publisher and editor gratefully acknowledge the assistance of the staff members and volunteers at the Washington National Cathedral, especially Richard T. Feller, Leonard W. Freeman, Charles A. Perry, Suzanne Pierron, and Jesse Wilson. They also wish to express their gratitude to the rector of Lynnwood Parish, Louis C. Breitenbach, for his help and support.

Passages from Holy Scripture are excerpted from The Holy Bible, *King James Version, Cambridge University Press.*

Photographs on pages 114-117 and drawings appear courtesy of the Washington National Cathedral.